RUBY E. DARE LIBRARY
College
62246
D0569977

CONTEMPORARY
SQUARE
DANCE

PHYSICAL EDUCATION ACTIVITIES SERIES

Consulting Editor:
AILEENE LOCKHART
University of Southern California
Los Angeles, California

Evaluation Materials Editor:
JANE A. MOTT
Smith College
Northampton, Massachusetts

793.34
P54

PHYSICAL EDUCATION
ACTIVITIES SERIES

CONTEMPORARY
SQUARE
DANCE

PATRICIA A. PHILLIPS
State College at Bridgewater
Bridgewater, Massachusetts

Illustrations by ROSALIE BROWN
Wheaton College
Norton, Massachusetts

WM. C. BROWN COMPANY PUBLISHERS
DUBUQUE, IOWA

Copyright © 1968 by
Wm. C. Brown Company Publishers

Library of Congress Catalog Card Number: 68–15375

ISBN 0–697–07008–5

All rights reserved. No part of this book may be
reproduced in any form or by any process without
permission in writing from the copyright owner.

Printed in the United States of America

Preface

Square dancing has been popular since early Colonial days, and its development has kept pace with the changing aspects of society in the United States. Square dancing requires skill, control, poise, physical and mental alertness, and quick reaction. Few activities offer greater opportunity for wider participation. This form of dance can be enjoyed and appreciated by participant and observer throughout a lifetime. It challenges all ages and all levels of ability; it can be as simple or as complex as desired. No expensive equipment is required.

This book is designed for the dancer who wishes to improve his skills and understandings. It should be used as a supplement to, not a substitute for, instruction and experience; the latter can be well reinforced and supported by the written word and by visual cues, but no amount of "reading about" square dancing can take the place of good instruction and direct, active participation.

The text presents a brief background of the development of this activity, but emphasis is placed chiefly on the fundamental skills and knowledges that are basic to good performance, that are representative of the skills which the reader will encounter, and that are necessary for the development of proficiency in the contemporary form of square dancing. Though planned primarily for the novice, it is believed that the experienced dancer will discover much of interest within these pages. Analyses of the basics are accompanied herein by numerous illustrations which should both illustrate the descriptions provided in the text and challenge the reader to compose his own figures, thus satisfying his creative abilities.

v

140543

Self-evaluation questions pertaining to both knowledge and skill are interspersed throughout these pages. These should provide the reader with examples of the kinds of understandings which he should be acquiring as he makes progress toward mastering the fundamentals of this universally enjoyed activity. The reader should try to respond to these questions as thoroughly and as adequately as possible, and should try his skill at developing additional ones to stimulate learning.

The author gratefully acknowledges the helpfulness of H. I. Tousignant, staff caller at Square Acres, East Bridgewater, Massachusetts, and Bob Trouchsler and Merle Silva Promenade Shop, Square Acres, in compiling dances for this book. Particular appreciation is expressed to Dick Leger, square dance caller and choreographer, Warren, Rhode Island, for his valuable criticism of the material.

Patricia A. Phillips

Contents

The Square Dance

What are the factors that induce so many people of all ages to participate so enthusiastically in square dancing? Why today do several million people in the United States still regularly attend square dances? To understand the reasons for this interest, the history and structure of the square dance should be considered.

During the very early development of what is now known as the Traditional Square Dance, very few basics (circle, do-sa-do, allemande left, and the like) were included in its structure. The visiting couple figure was the predominant formation used. Couple number one, for example, "visited" couple number two and performed one or two fundamentals, then visited couple number three and then four, where the same movements were repeated. If a couple were unfamiliar with the figure, this man and lady could take couple number four position, and by the time they were involved in the dance, they would understand what was expected of them. The dance was uncomplicated, but its very simplicity provided the relaxation these people sought. The pleasure of dancing came from the companionship of friends and the mutual enjoyment of the rhythm, melody, and the singing which accompanied the activity, not from the mastery of complicated steps or patterns or from the intellectual stimulation of unexpected calls.

A boisterous element arose during the early stage of the development of the dance which caused some unrest. The esthetic aspect of the dance was not of interest to some persons. They enjoyed the foot stomping, hand clapping, and "skipping around the set" which they introduced. The square dance in some places became even a "hay-seed, hip-flask carrying" activity.

The effects of this "barn dance era" are still felt today. Some people, never having attended a square dance, think of this form of dance as a "free-for-all." This could not be further from the truth.

The Traditional Square Dancers, those truly interested in preserving the dance in its early American form, broke away from this group and formed their own "clubs." Some of the dances they still perform are intricate and beautiful in construction and footwork. In order to participate in this highly developed dance form, it is necessary to spend a great amount of time learning to perform the many complicated and coordinated movements often associated with it and in memorizing the order of these movements. Because some of these dances require precise timing and the mastery of difficult manuevers, it is not possible for people to participate as informally and as quickly as they did in the visiting couple figure of the early days. People of today should be grateful to the Traditional Square Dancers who have preserved those beautiful dances whose history is linked with the development of this country. One should appreciate the cultural values inherent in this dance form. Its very formation and structure suggest the people who originally developed it. Participants move from one set of couples to the next, enjoying their performance of certain precise skills which require good timing and the cooperation of all. Each person is accepted because he is an integral part of the total group and because he can contribute to the enjoyment of others. Each attends because he is sincerely interested in dance as an art form and because he enjoys good dancing. Courtesy and goodwill characterize the participants. These same attitudes continue to prevail in the dance as it is performed today.

Few changes were made in the square dance until the period of World War II. During this time, the pace of living increased and more challenge was sought, consistent with the changing concepts and heightened activity of the period. The square dance as it existed did not satisfy the people of that time. The visiting couple figure left too much time in inactivity. This generation wanted a dance which would adhere to correct timing and phrasing but which would actively involve everyone at the same time. This impatient generation did not want to spend the time required to learn specific, prechoreographed, traditional dances. They wanted a dance in which they could participate readily. They also wanted music which was up-to-date, played by a band which made use of more popular new instrumentation and orchestration.

In California during the mid-1940's, grid work (posting) was developed. One set of couples (two couples) were activiated; the inactive couples were used as guide posts and, around them, the active couples move in and out of the set. Soon, new basics were introduced as were

2

new formations. The singing call (a dance written for a specific melody) was still popular but the hash call became equally as popular. (The hash call is a dance which is not memorized by the dancers. It is not limited to a set number of beats but can continue indefinitely at the caller's discretion. He choreographs the dance. His calls *direct,* not merely accompany, the dance.) Up to this time, after having memorized some twenty or thirty dances, a caller was considered sufficiently proficient to handle an entire evening of square dancing. With the advent of the hash call, memorization of figures alone was not sufficient preparation to call a dance. Now the caller must, of course, memorize a wide repertoire of singing calls, and he must know many dances chosen from the thousands which have been written. A caller today must also have spent several years studying the innumerable basics now involved in the dance. He must know what each is capable of accomplishing and how to combine them into interesting figures. He must know the timing for each, and he must develop certain techniques for introducing them and for teaching the throngs of people who now crowd the square dance clubs and halls. He must keep up with the two or three new basics which become popular each year, and he should be familiar with the latest releases.

The great changes in the square dance began in the West and slowly made their way to the East, showing up there around the mid-1950's. People were attracted to the dance because of these changes and also because of the attitude prevailing among the avid dancers—the love for good dancing and the courtesy which was originally displayed in the Traditional Square Dance. The Contemporary Square Dance necessitates good coordination, mental alertness, good rhythm, and smooth, graceful movement. Gone are the jumping, skipping, and hopping found in the barn dance. Gone too are the foot-stomping and hand clapping.

Reference is sometimes made to the Western Square Dance. As the latest changes in the dance began in the West, this term was once used to differentiate the "new" dance from the Traditional. After the changes filtered through the entire United States, the term "Modern" came into existence. Today the Western Square Dance denotes a particular type of tune (Western). Westerners also enjoy a faster tempo and sometimes perform certain basics in fewer beats than do the Easterners. The terms "Traditional" and "Modern" or "Contemporary" are now used to differentiate the two main types of square dance performed in the United States today.

In the Modern Square Dance, the more popular tunes of the 1960's as well as those from the 1920's, 1930's, and on, are utilized in the singing call. Participants enjoy dancing to these tunes recorded by bands which employ the Dixieland, Tijuana Brass, or Latin sounds. The approach

How can you distinguish among these terms: Barn Dance, Traditional Square Dance, Western Square Dance, Modern Square Dance?

Evaluation Question

to learning is vastly different. Participants in the Modern Square Dance do not memorize dances as such. This would be an impossibility as so many have been published. After having learned the basics, dancers are capable of performing any dance which contains these elements even though the dancers never heard of the specific dance before.

The square dance is part of the culture of the people in the United States. It is, therefore, a growing, developing activity characteristic of these people. The Traditional Square Dance should be studied by the student who is concerned with the evolution and history of culture in this country. Since Modern Square Dance is a dynamic activity indicative of the changing culture of people of this country, it too is of interest to the student of today for this *is* the square dance of people of this nation at this time in history. One need not be an historian, however, to enjoy this physically and mentally challenging, fast-moving, infectiously interesting activity—Modern Square Dancing!

Information
for the Beginning
Square Dancer

In order to participate in the Modern Square Dance, several terms must be understood.

TERMINOLOGY

Basic

A basic is a fundamental skill, such as the circle, do-sa-do, or ladies chain, which is directed to all of the dancers or to a set of couples. It is necessary to use a specific number of beats in order to execute each basic correctly. At no time should dancers have to resort to undue rushing in order to complete a movement. Throughout the United States, almost every basic is performed with a uniform timing. It is possible, therefore, to judge the number of steps required and to understand the spatial patterns through which these steps should move the dancers.

Figure

A figure is comprised of several basics which have been arranged in a specific and meaningful order. In a figure, a set of couples weaves around the square until the couples, or at least the men, are back in their home positions. The ladies, if out of position, will return to home position if the figure is repeated once or three times.

Hoedown Record

A hoedown record has a definite repetitive beat but very little melody. A teacher or caller uses only a four- to six-note range in calling

On which beat of this phrase should the caller begin? Can you do the shuffle step in the rhythm indicated by these notes?

Evaluation Questions

KEEPING TIME

the directions for the dance and in chattering or syllabalizing on every beat. This is known as "patter calling." Square dancing is performed to lively 2/4, 4/4, and, very occasionally, 6/8 music. In a hoedown record, the first beat of every eight-beat phrase is heavily accented while the first beat of the second four of the eight-beat group is less heavily accented. When a caller begins to call, he does so on the first or, preferably, on the fifth beat of the phrase. As the caller directs the dance, he must adhere to this conventionality so that the dancers will move with the musical phrasing. Most elementary basics require eight to sixteen beats. Since there is the definite beat at the beginning of each eight-beat phrase, the caller need not count each beat consciously; rather, he uses his feel and musical senses for direction.

A hoedown record is used when learning square dance fundamentals. The continuous definite rhythm and the absence of a clearly defined melody make learning comparatively simple. The hoedown record is also used for the hash call. In this particular type of dance, the caller makes use of his ingenuity and skill to compose figures; this he does by combining basics into interesting combinations. The figures may last any number of beats. To keep intermediate and advanced dancers attentive and concentrating, most callers use a basic figure for one dance but then add many other basics and variations to offset the actual design of the figure. The hash call is not memorized, so dancers have no idea what will be called next. Most square dancers enjoy "hash" for it challenges their ability to listen, their knowledge of the basics, and their ability to react accurately with good coordination and timing.

Diagram A:

KEEPING TIME

Singing Call Record

A singing call record has a definite melody; the specific directions for specific dance figures are sung to this melody. Most singing call records are composed of a melody which takes 64 beats to complete. There are usually seven groups of 64 beats. The author writes two figures for this dance. One figure is executed by starting and ending with the same partner. The other figure ordinarily is used to exchange partners. The usual order for the appearance of these two figures is:

Figure one	1st group of 64 beats (the opening)
Figure two	2nd group of 64 beats
Figure two	3rd group of 64 beats
Figure one	4th group of 64 beats (the middle)
Figure two	5th group of 64 beats
Figure two	6th group of 64 beats
Figure one	7th group of 64 beats (the closing)

It is possible to have six groups of 72 beats and five groups of 80 beats. In each case, two figures usually are used, the main figure appearing four times and the other at the beginning and ending (six groups of 72) or in the middle (five groups of 80 beats).

Tip

A tip is a group of dances called consecutively without a break. In many sections of the country, a tip consists of one hash call (or patter call) plus one singing call. Although the tip is defined differently in some sections, this is the most generally accepted meaning.

Which of these arm positions does a man assume as he moves around the set? Which is most usual? Least usual?

Evaluation Questions

THE MAN'S ARM POSITION

THE MUSIC BEGINS

Forming Sets

Most teachers and callers begin a lesson or a tip by playing a hoedown record. This indicates to the dancers that the leader is ready to begin. Dancers should immediately choose partners and form sets. A couple should take a place on the floor and hold up three fingers, thus indicating that three additional couples are needed to complete the set. As couples join, the number of additional couples needed to complete the set is indicated in the same manner.

Numbering Couples in the Set

Number three couple

Number four couple   Number two couple

Number one couple

(Couple number one always has its back to the caller)

Position of Partner and Corner

The man's partner is always on his right, and his corner on his left. The lady's partner is always on her left and her corner on her right. The man's opposite is always the lady directly across the set from him, and the lady's opposite is the gentleman straight across from her. These positions must be completely understood. Failure to react automatically to these positions will result in many mistakes. In square dancing, original partners may find themselves separated by the entire set. At the word

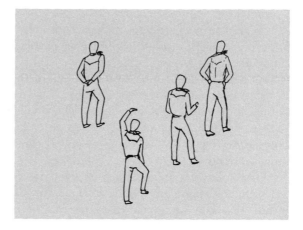

Diagram B:

THE MAN'S ARM
POSITION

"partner," however, the man turns to his right, the lady to her left, and the person so encountered at that moment becomes the partner. The term "partner" and "corner" denote *position* or *direction*.

Dance Step

A shuffle step is taken with each beat of the music . . . a light shuffle on the balls of the feet; the feet are barely lifted from the floor between steps. One *never* hops, skips, jumps, runs, or leaps around the set.

Styling

When standing in the set, the man should always hold the lady's hand. His elbow is bent and his hand, with palm facing the ceiling, is slightly higher than the level of his elbow. The lady places her hand on top of his. Hands are not held, rather palm rests upon palm.

Stamping the feet and clapping the hands are taboo. To do so is a marked discourtesy to the caller, to the teacher, and to the other dancers; instruction or calls cannot be given or heard above this clamor.

When moving around the set, the lady should have both hands, or her free hand, on her skirt and should flare it out in relation to her movements. The beauty of the dance comes not only from the movement but from the styling as well. When moving around the set, the men usually keep their arms at their sides, elbows bent slightly. The hands are parallel and in front of the body. In some sections of the country, the men clasp their hands behind them or place them on their hips. These latter positions are, however, slowly disappearing in order to leave the dancer prepared for the hand turns.

9

Timing

In order to execute each basic correctly, a definite number of beats are required. The student should give particular attention to this aspect of the dance. As dancers acquire more ability, successful completion of a figure depends also upon exact timing in the execution of the figure. It is extremely important that dancers not anticipate calls in the contemporary form of the square dance. The teacher or caller gives each basic the necessary number of beats when he calls it. The dancers should react only *after* the call has been given. If this response is made, all will move correctly.

The following information is given in a call: the people who are to perform, the name of the basic, and the direction of performance if it is one that can be executed either left or right. For instance: "All join hands and circle left."

> all—designates the performers
> circle—indicates the basic
> left—gives the direction

As it takes eight beats to perform this basic halfway around the set and as the information just described takes only four beats to call, four beats must be added to the call in order to make up the required number of beats. This is accomplished by adding four beats of "patter." This may be a rhyming couplet or a repetition of the call itself. The caller will begin the first call either on the first or (preferably) on the fifth, sixth, seventh or eighth beat of the phrase. After the call "All join hands and circle left," the dancers will begin; thus, they will start on the fifth beat of an eight-beat phrase or on the first beat of the phrase. The better callers phrase their calls in such a way that the dancers can begin dancing on the first beat of the succeeding phrase. It is more difficult to call the dance this way, but this construction makes for better and truly correct dancing. If the caller is precise, dancers need not count out each step required to execute a basic; if they begin after the call has been given, they will automatically move with the phrasing of the music. Eventually, dancers will encounter manuevers which require only two or four beats. Since the calls for the execution of these basics will come so quickly, dancers must not anticipate calls but must *listen* carefully and respond *after* each call has been given.

Occasionally, a caller may give several calls, one after the other without any intervening patter. (He would not do this unless he was certain that the dancers were sufficiently advanced to follow him.) He may do this to give himself time to sing the lyrics of the song to which the specific dance was written. For instance:

Allemande left your corner	4 beats	requires	8 beats
Do-sa-do your own	4 beats	requires	8 beats
Promenade your corner	4 beats		
All the way to home	4 beats	requires	16 beats
	16 beats		32 beats

No patter was used above. In all, sixteen beats were used in the call though 32 are required for performance. After "Promenade your corner all the way to home," the caller must utilize 16 beats in patter or in calling the lyric to the song if his timing is to be correct and if he is to provide the time required by the dancers to execute his calls. Dancers must utilize the appropriate number of beats which each basic demands while remembering their sequence.

The number of steps needed to travel in various directions around the set follows:

1. Four steps to walk across the set.
2. Eight steps to travel halfway around the set in a circle formation; sixteen steps to complete the entire circle.
3. Four steps make a hand turn or courtesy turn.

Analysis of the hand turn: To travel the distance to one's corner requires four steps (one quarter of the distance of the set). If both dancers travel toward each other at the same time, however, the distance and the time required to reach one's partner is cut in half; thus, two steps are taken. Using this information, one can now analyze the allemande left, for example: To move toward the corner, two steps are taken, the hand turn requires four steps, to walk back to the original position requires two steps. The allemande left, then, requires eight beats to execute.

The position of the dancers in a set also determines the number of beats required to execute a call. For instance, the right and left thru combines two movements: First, the dancers walk across the set (four steps), and then make a courtesy turn (four steps). If this call is directed to the head couples, starting from home position, eight steps will be taken in performing this movement. Suppose, however, that couple one is facing couple two, an arm's length away, and the same call is directed to them. In this case, the dancers will not move the complete distance across the set, thus only six beats are given—two to pass each other and four to perform the courtesy turn.

This information is given to the student in order that he might appreciate the complexity of the square dance. The caller not only has to combine basics into interesting spatial combinations, but he must do so simultaneously with reference to proper temporal organization and with reference to the position of the dancers in the set. In addition, continuous movement must be maintained throughout the dance. At no time should dancers be still when involved in performing a figure. Movement should flow and continue without hesitation. Thus, calls should be made *before* they are to be executed.

The question of timing is sometimes a controversial subject among callers. It is possible, of course, to analyze precisely the number of beats required to execute each basic when the set is uniform in size. However, since the dance is composed of a combination of basics (a series of movements flowing from one to the next), the timing of each basic should also be analyzed in accordance with the position of the dancers in the set and with reference to the basic which precedes and follows it. The controversy among callers arises with reference to the total combination. "Are certain beats part of a particular basic or are those beats part of the basic which came before or after it?" The beginning student need not concern himself with such technicalities. He should, however, be aware that each basic does require a certain number of beats for its performance and that callers the country over recognize this fact though they may analyze the required beats differently. The author has indicated in this book the time which is required for the actual performance of each basic without reference to the differing numbers of steps which are necessary from the various positions from which the basic may be performed. Since callers have different opinions on this matter, the analysis given here may not necessarily meet with the unanimous approval of all callers.

LEARNING TO SQUARE DANCE

Professional callers instruct dancers in the mechanics of executing the basics of Modern Square Dancing. They build on the dancers' knowledge until they know enough to perform a dance. For instance, the circle and do-sa-do may be explained and then called in various patterns. Once these have been learned, another fundamental is introduced in the same way, and so on, until the dancers have mastered many basics and formations. This approach is used to insure that the dancers actually have learned these fundamentals and are not merely memorizing figures. The dancers must learn to listen attentively. They will learn that basics can be arranged in many patterns. The sense of accomplishment that dancers receive from performing a dance correctly even though they never heard of it before is one of the great aspects of the Modern Square Dance. The participants learn basics, but they rely on their sense of timing, their coordination, their mental ability, their group endeavor, and the timing of the caller's directions to perform a figure which they have not memorized.

In contrast, due to the intricacies of some of the figures and footwork involved in the Traditional Square Dance, memorization of dances is often a necessity. In addition, basics are not always called out as descriptively in the Traditional as they are in the Modern Square Dance. This construction often demands that dancers know specific dances and have memorized the sequence of their basics. Traditional square dancers place emphasis chiefly on the beauty of the dance. Styling, smooth graceful movement coordinated with the rhythm and construction of the music, and precision of footwork are the most important aspects of this dance.

Whether one learns by the memorization method or by the method employed by callers of the Modern Square Dance, he should have two major objectives in mind: (1) to strive for perfection of movement, in styling and in the timing of the basics and figures in relation to the music and (2) to concentrate on learning basics.

Considering that there are nearly 200 basics, obviously concentration, alertness, good coordination, and rhythm are required in order to participate in this activity successfully. Each dancer must fully understand the makeup and function of each fundamental. Whether these are introduced by the modern method or in a figure or dance, the concept of the basic itself is the same. By combining basics, many different figures can be made; if each is understood, it can be performed regardless of the sequence in which it may be found.

The student should carefully analyze each fundamental as it is introduced. In which direction does one move? Which hand is used to execute the turn? When could this be called? Most important, what does it accomplish—where will the dancers be at the conclusion? Each lesson should be approached with such questions in mind.

HOW TO STUDY THE FOLLOWING CHAPTERS

In the following chapters, basics are presented in a progression. After each is defined, a pattern or figure is presented which makes use of the basic. The figure begins and ends with the dancers at home position or with original partners back together again. In those cases where only one set of couples (heads or sides) are activated, the author has used only the heads in working the figure through. The same figure, of course, can be performed by the sides.

The student should follow the action of the dancers while studying each figure. In the "posting" section (Chapter Five), it will be found advantageous to follow number one man. When he is brought back to his home position, all other dancers will be home also. In Chapter Seven (line or route formation), the student should visualize the position of couple number one in relation to couples two and four.

If the student follows the action of the dancers, it will be possible to read part of the figure, to stop and see where number one man is at that point, or where couple number one is in relation to two and four. When this has been accomplished, the student will be well on his way to developing a good grasp of square dance compositions.

In Chapter Three only, the number of beats required for the execution of each basic in the figures is presented. This information is needed only by the caller and therefore is not included in subsequent chapters. During a dancer's introduction to square dancing, however, he should learn the number of steps needed to travel from one side of the set to the other, halfway around the set, and to make hand turns. The spatial sense so developed should carry through into the performance of all other basics.

Diagrammatic illustrations are included to give the student a clear picture of what is accomplished by the execution of the more difficult fundamentals. The squares represent the men; the circles represent the ladies. The points in the drawings indicate the direction that the men and women are facing. Number one man and woman are darkened in the diagrams so that they may be distinguished easily from the other dancers. In studying each diagram, follow number one man to learn what each basic accomplishes.

3

Elementary Basics
Used in the Traditional
and the Modern
Square Dance

To develop proficiency in square dancing, it is extremely important to thoroughly learn some fundamental movements.

ELEMENTARY BASICS

Circle (8 beats to go halfway around; 16 all the way around)

Men bend their elbows so that their hands are slightly above the level of their elbows, palms facing upward. Ladies place their hands on the men's hands. All turn slightly in the direction indicated by the call. Circle in that direction. The circle may be performed half way or all the way around the set.

Call:	All join hands and circle left	4 beats
Patter:	Circle left around the set	4 beats = 8 beats
Call:	All join hands and circle right	4 beats
Patter:	Circle right go all the way	4 beats
Patter:	All the way around the set	4 beats
Patter:	Circle right around you bet	4 beats = 16 beats

Do-Sa-Do (8 beats)

Walk toward the person indicated, passing right shoulders with that person. Move sidewards to the right and, passing left shoulders, back up to the original position.

Call:	Do-sa-do your corner	4 beats
Patter:	Your corner do-sa-do	4 beats = 8 beats

15

Ladies Chain (8 beats—4 to walk across and 4 to courtesy turn)

The two ladies indicated walk toward each other, touch right hands. They do not form a star. In most sections of the country, women flare their skirts into the center and do not touch hands, walk by, and extend left hand to the man each is facing. They perform a courtesy turn. The man takes the lady's left hand in his left hand. Placing right arm around her waist, he turns her to his left until both face the center of the set. While the women walk across the set, the men take two steps back, then two steps forward (equalling the four steps the women take to cross the set) to meet the lady coming toward them.

| **Call:** | Head two ladies chain across | 4 beats | |
| **Patter:** | Chain across the ring and then | 4 beats $=$ 8 beats | |

| **Call:** | Head two ladies chain right back | 4 beats | |
| **Patter:** | Chain right back across the track | 4 beats $=$ 8 beats | |

The ladies chain may be executed by all four ladies or by chaining to the right or to the left of the set.

All Four Ladies Chain (8 beats)

The ladies walk into the center, place their right hands so that all hands are touching. Turn to the left and walk around until the opposite man is reached. As only four beats are given to reach this man, the ladies must not take too much time placing their hands together in the middle. Moving to the left and reaching the opposite man is the purpose. When he is reached, a courtesy turn is executed.

| **Call:** | All four ladies chain across | 4 beats | |
| **Patter:** | Turn the girls and don't get lost | 4 beats $=$ 8 beats | |

Head (Side) Ladies Chain to the Right (or Left) (8 beats)

The two head ladies chain with the ladies on their right. As this call is given, the side ladies move to their left. Number one lady chains with number two lady. Number three lady chains with number four. When the two head ladies chain back, all will be in their original positions. "Head ladies chain to the left"—number one chains with number four; number three with number two.

| **Call:** | Head two ladies chain to the right | 4 beats | |
| **Patter:** | Turn the girls and hold on tight | 4 beats $=$ 8 beats | |

| **Call:** | Head two ladies chain right back | 4 beats | |
| **Patter:** | Chain right back and turn like that | 4 beats $=$ 8 beats | |

16

Evaluation Questions

How many beats does it take to do-sa-do your partner? To go forward and back? To promenade your corner?

Promenade (8 beats halfway; 16 all the way)

Partners face counterclockwise, side by side, with the man on the inside of the ring. The man places both of his hands in front of the lady. She places both of her hands in his (left to left, right to right). Both walk around the set. The promenade may be performed by just the ladies, by just the men, or by one set of couples. If performed by the ladies, they walk to their right (counterclockwise) around the inside of the set. The men should react in the same manner. If the head (or side) couples are called, usually the call indicates moving to the outside of the ring and halfway around the set to take the opposite position from which they started.

Following are a group of figures utilizing the 64 beats usually found in the singing call. These figures contain the circle, do-sa-do, ladies chain, and promenade.

1. All join hands and circle left   8 beats
   Circle right the other way back   8 beats
   Do-sa-do the corner   8 beats
   Do-sa-do the partner   8 beats
   Circle left go all the way around   16 beats
   Promenade go round to home   16 beats = 64 beats

2. Head two ladies chain across   8 beats
   Head two ladies chain right back   8 beats
   Side two ladies chain across   8 beats
   Side two ladies chain right back   8 beats
   Do-sa-do the corner   8 beats

Do-sa-do the partner	8 beats
Promenade the corner	16 beats = 64 beats

3. | | |
|---|---|
| All join hands and circle left (halfway) | 8 beats |
| All four ladies chain | 8 beats |
| All four ladies chain back | 8 beats |
| All join hands and circle right | 8 beats |
| Do-sa-do your corner | 8 beats |
| Do-sa-do your partner | 8 beats |
| Promenade your corner | 16 beats = 64 beats |

4. | | |
|---|---|
| Head two ladies chain to the right | 8 beats |
| Head two ladies chain back | 8 beats |
| Head two ladies chain to the left | 8 beats |
| Head two ladies chain back | 8 beats |
| All join hands and circle right (halfway) | 8 beats |
| Do-sa-do the corner | 8 beats |
| Do-sa-do the partner | 8 beats |
| Promenade the corner | 8 beats = 64 beats |

Allemande Left (8 beats)

This is usually performed with the corner. Facing the corner and joining left hands, dancers walk around each other to face in the opposite direction. They then walk back toward their partner. The allemande left is usually proceeded by a basic which involves the partner. The forearm grip for hand turns is used in most sections of the country (holding onto the forearm of the other person, each dancer pulls in toward his own body while leaning away from the pull. By making use of the other dancer's strength, balance, and resistance, a sustained, graceful, easy turn should result). When the allemande left has been completed, partners should be facing each other. If the call "allemande left" is not preceded or succeeded by a designated person, it is understood that reference is made to the corner.

Call:	Allemande left the corner	4 beats
Patter:	Your corner allemande left	4 beats = 8 beats

Figure using the allemande left:

Allemande left the corner	8 beats
Do-sa-do partner	8 beats
Circle left halfway	8 beats
Allemande left	8 beats

Do-sa-do partner	8 beats
Four ladies chain	8 beats
Four ladies chain back	8 beats
Promenade to home	8 beats = 64 beats

Grand Right and Left (8 beats halfway)

Facing partners, dancers join right hands and walk by. Extend left hand to the next and walk by, right hand to the next and walk by, left to the next, walk by, and the right hand should then be free to meet one's partner. The men always move counterclockwise around the set, the women, clockwise (A grand right and left completely around the set is seldom performed in the Modern Square Dance but is used quite often in the Traditional Square Dance.)

Call:	Grand right and left go round the set	4 beats
Patter:	Halfway around with a grand right and left	4 beats = 8 beats

Figure using the grand right and left:

Allemande left	8 beats
Grand right and left	8 beats
Do-sa-do partner	8 beats
Allemande left	8 beats
Grand right and left	8 beats
Do-sa-do partner (all should now be in home positions)	8 beats
Promenade all the way	16 beats = 64 beats

Weave the Ring

This call merely indicates a grand right and left without hand clasps.

Forward and Back (8 beats)

The couples designated by the call (their inside hands are joined) walk forward four steps into the center of the set, then back to place with four steps. On the fourth forward step, the dancers usually clap the free hand with the person opposite.

Call:	Head two couples forward and back	4 beats
Patter:	Up and back like that	4 beats = 8 beats

19

Figure using forward and back:

Head two couples forward and back	8 beats
Head two ladies chain	8 beats
Side two couples forward and back	8 beats
Side two ladies chain	8 beats
All four ladies chain across	8 beats
Allemande left	8 beats
Promenade all the way	16 beats = 64 beats

Right and Left Thru (8 beats)

The two designated couples walk forward, touch the right hand of the opposite person, walk by, passing right shoulders with that person. As soon as the couples have passed each other, the man takes his partner's left hand in his left hand, and they perform a courtesy turn.

Call:	Head two couples right and left thru	4 beats
Patter:	Turn the girl around you do	4 beats = 8 beats

Couples are now on the opposite side of the set. Repeating the call will bring the couples back to original position. This may also be performed with the couples on the right and on the left.

Call:	Heads to the right with a right and left thru	4 beats
Patter:	Turn the girl around you do	4 beats = 8 beats

Figure using right and left thru:

Head two couples right and left thru	8 beats
Side two couples right and left thru	8 beats
Head two couples right and left thru	8 beats
Side two couples right and left thru	8 beats
Allemande left	8 beats
Grand right and left	8 beats
Do-sa-do partner	8 beats
Promenade corner	8 beats = 64 beats

Star, Right Hand and Left Hand (8 beats)

The designated persons move into the center and join hands as indicated by the call (right hand for a right hand star, and left hand for a left hand star). Grasping the wrist of the person ahead, walk forward.

Call:	Men star right in the middle tonight	4 beats
Patter:	Once around and hold on tight	4 beats = 8 beats

If the men star right, a do-sa-do with the partner cannot be called to finish this basic because the men in this case will be facing their partners from the wrong direction. Usually the caller directs the men to pass by their partners and execute an allemande left with their corners in order to bring them back to their partners. If the men star left, they will be in the correct position to perform a do-sa-do with their partners.

Figures using the star:

(1)	Men star left	8 beats
	Do-sa-do the partner	8 beats
	Ladies promenade inside	8 beats
	Allemande left the corner	8 beats
	Grand right and left	8 beats
	Do-sa-do the partner	8 beats
	Allemande left the corner	8 beats
	Promenade	8 beats = 64 beats
(2)	Men star right pass partner by	8 beats
	Allemande left the corner	8 beats
	Do-sa-do the partner	8 beats
	Ladies promenade inside	8 beats
	Allemande left the corner	8 beats
	Do sa do the partner	8 beats
	Promenade your own	16 beats = 64 beats

HEADS (SIDES) STAR RIGHT

Star Left with Sides (Heads) Into the Middle Star Right (24 beats—8 to star right in the center, 8 to star with the sides, 8 to star in the center again)

Head couples walk into the center and star by the right one full turn around. They walk toward their corners and star by the left with the sides one full turn around. The sides stay in original position while the heads travel into the center and star by the right once more. (This was described previously. Instead of the men or the women making the

21

From this position, can you combine basics to bring all dancers back to home position in 32 beats?

Evaluation Question
COMBINING BASICS

star, couples do so. Because this is sometimes difficult to comprehend, this description is included.)

Call:	Head two couples star by the right	4 beats
Patter:	Once around in the middle tonight	4 beats
Call:	Star by the left with the outside two	4 beats
Patter:	Once around the ring you do	4 beats
Call:	Into the middle with a right hand star	4 beats
Patter:	Once around but not too far	4 beats = 24 beats

Figure using the star left with sides:

All join hands and circle left all the way	16 beats
Head couples star by the right	8 beats
Star by the left with the sides	8 beats
Star right in the middle	8 beats
Allemande left	8 beats
Grand right and left	8 beats
Promenade partner	8 beats = 64 beats

Star Promenade

While the men are performing a left-hand star, the caller may say, "Pick up your partner, arm around, star promenade." As each man moves

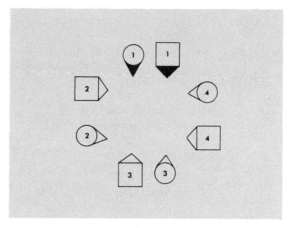

Diagram C:

COMBINING BASICS

by his partner, he puts his right arm around her waist, while still maintaining the left-hand star. This results in the star promenade position, and the dancers continue to move around the set. The caller has the option of holding the star promenade as long as he desires. When he wishes to terminate it, he may call, "Hub back out and roll promenade." The men then drop the left-hand star, while still holding their partners, and back out of the star, completely around. This call is followed immediately by another call such as "Promenade her home."

While in the star promenade, the call may be given, "Ladies back track go the other way around." The men then drop the ladies' hands. The ladies turn to their right to face in the opposite direction and proceed to promenade, individually, in that direction. "Pass her once, meet again, turn her by the right hand (same as allemande left but performed with right hand), turn corner by the left (allemande left), back to the partner. . . ."

Swing (8 beats)

In performing this basic, the buzz step is used throughout most of the country. Partners take a closed dance position. The outside of the right foot is placed fairly close to the partner's right foot. Partners lean back away from each other at the same time, maintaining a slight pull toward each other with the arms. Partners pivot on the right foot, pushing with the left. The swing is often considered to be the most beautiful movement in the square dance. The woman, however, can easily lose her balance because of the turning movement; therefore, the man must exert his strength in controlling his partner. If he does not, couples may find themselves bumping into each other.

Call:	Swing your partner round and round	4 beats
Patter:	Swing that lady off the ground	4 beats = 8 beats

Figure using the swing:

Allemande left	8 beats
Grand right and left	8 beats
Meet your partner, swing	8 beats
Join hands circle left	8 beats
Allemande left	8 beats
Swing your own	8 beats
Promenade her home	16 beats = 64 beats

SELECTED DANCES CONTAINING THOSE BASICS INTRODUCED IN CHAPTER 3

A selected list of dances containing those basics introduced in this section follows.

Windsor

4415	Coming Round the Mountain	Doc Alumbaugh
4814	On the Trail of the Lonesome Pine	Don Armstrong
4144B	Just Because	
4112B	Marching Through Georgia	
4405	Old Fashioned Girl	Paul Phillips

Blue Star

1581	Pickles	Vaughn Parrish
1681	Tie Me Kangaroo Down	Andy Andrus

Top

25003	Marina	Dick Leger

Kimbo,
  U.S.A.

Educational Records	Modern Square Dance Album	Dick Leger
		Patricia Phillips
4060		

4

Basics Used
in the Traditional
Square Dance

The Traditional Square Dance, if contras and quadrilles are included, contains many intricate movements. This section could never do justice to the knowledge needed by dancers to participate in this dance successfully. For this reason, only those basics are presented which are most often encountered. It should be noted that while these basics originated with the Traditional Square Dance, many are utilized also in the contemporary version of this dance form. As the visiting couple figure is used more frequently in the elementary stage, this formation is utilized in the following examples.

1. First couple bow and swing
   Lead to the right of the ring (to couple number two) (perform basics such as do-sa-do, ladies chain, and the like)
   Lead to the next couple (couple number three) (perform the same sequence of basics)
   Lead to the next couple (couple number four)
   Go back home to swing or allemande left
2. Same type of figure as in number one but a different sequence of basics is used as each new couple is visited
3. First couple go right and circle four (lead to couple two)
   Leave that lady go on to the next (number one man leaves his lady with number two and goes alone to couple number three)
   Take that lady and lead to the next couple (four)
   Leave that lady (number two lady is left with man number four)
   Go back home

Number one and number three men are left standing alone while number four and number two men have a lady on either side of them. Each man, however, still has his own partner on his right side even though men one and three do not have them by the hand. Several basics could be included for the two lines of three and for the single men. When finished, partners can be found by merely going from an allemande left back to partner or by simply swinging the lady on the right (partner).

4. Head couples forward and back
   Right and left thru
   Head couples circle four
   Two ladies chain
   Chain back
   Head couples right and left thru
   Allemande left
   Swing your own

(Only one set of couples performs while the other couples remain inactive. When the figure ends, the remaining couples perform the same sequence.)

BASICS AND TERMINOLOGY USED IN THE TRADITIONAL SQUARE DANCE

Around Your Own the Other Way Home (8 beats)
   When partners meet in a grand right and left, they clasp right hands, walk around until facing in the reverse direction (for grand right and left). They perform another grand right and left back to home position.

   Call: Allemande left with your left hand
   Right to your own and then
   Grand right and left go round the ring
   Keep going until you meet again
   Around your own the other way home
   Keep going until you're home

Birdie in the Cage (8 beats)
   The active partners usually perform this. Form a circle of four (or any number), the lady walks into the center and the rest circle around her.

Crow Flies In (8 beats)
   The man walks into the center and the rest circle around him.

Call: First couple right and circle four
Circle four halfway around
Birdie in the cage and circle once
Circle once around
Now the crow flies in and the bird flies out
Circle four hands round
Crow flies out and everyone swing

Break That Ring

This term is used merely to indicate that hands are dropped in the circle or star formation. The call is followed by a swing, hand turn, or promenade.

Buckle Up Two

This is a term used to designate that hands are joined in a circle formation, for example, "Head two ladies buckle up two, circle once around."

Chassé (8 beats)

This designates a slide step: step-close, step-close. If the call is to "Chassé by your partner and come back again," the men take one step back and three slide steps to the right, then back to the left, finishing with one step forward. The ladies take three slide steps to the left and three to the right.

Half Sashay (4 beats)

The lady moves in front of her partner, the man behind. An exchange of partners has been made. Occasionally, "Roll away, half sashay" is called in which case the men pull on the ladies' left hand with their right. The ladies turn to face the men and continue turning until they are on the left of the men. An exchange of partners has thus been made with this call.

Circle Once and a Half (12 beats)

Circle one full turn plus a half more.

Call: First couple lead to the right
Join up hands and circle
Circle once and a half
Once and a half and go no more
Now dive thru into the center
Swing your lady around

27

Cross Over (4 beats; in Traditional Dances, sometimes 8 beats)

The designated dancers walk across the set and stand in the opposite position.

Call: Head two men cross over
And stand beside that Miss

Do-Si-Do

Same as do-sa-do.

Duck for the Oyster (8 beats), *Dive for the Clam* (8 beats)

The designated couples walk to the couple on their right, join hands with them and circle to the left halfway. With hands joined, the designated couple passes under the raised hands of the visited couple taking three steps forward and back. The designated couple now makes the arch for the other couple and the same procedure follows (Dive for the Clam). Another arch is now made by the visited couple, and the active couple passes under it to proceed to the next couple.

Call: First couple lead to the right
Circle half around
Duck for the oyster, in you go
Now back right up and don't be slow
Duck for the clam—under and then
Back right up as quick as you can
Now dive again and lead to the next

Duck and Dive (16 beats from the start of the duck under until the active couple, number one, leads to the right to face the next couple).

Couple number one joins hands with couple number two and circles halfway around. Couple one is now on the outside of the set. Couples drop hands at the call "Duck and Dive," couple two makes an arch and moves forward to home position, turning around, while couple number one walks under the arch. Couple one is then facing couple four and makes an arch. Couple four moves under the arch while couple one walks forward to couple four's position and then turns around. Couple four makes the arch for couple two to walk under. Couple four turns around immediately after this. Couple two makes the arch for couple one, and so on, until couples two and four are back in their home positions and couple one is in the center of the set.

Call: First couple lead to the right
Circle half then duck and dive

Under you go, then over again
Turn on around, then duck under
Over you go, then turn on around
Duck under and lead to the right

Eight Hands Across
All four couples walk into the center to join hands.

Call: Eight hands across and circle left
        Circle left halfway

Grand Allemande (32 beats halfway; 64 all the way around)
The designated dancers hook right elbows, turn once and a quarter, and take the next person by the left elbow to turn once and a quarter. This is repeated with each person until the next basic is called.

Grapevine Twist (20 beats, if circle left is included)
The first couple, inside hands joined, walk in between the couple on their right (couple two) with the man in the lead; then around the second lady and back into the center of the set. Making a clockwise turn, they proceed to walk through couple two again, but this time around the man. These couples now join hands and circle to the left once around.

Call: First couple lead to the right
        For a grapevine twist
        First gent around that lady
        Back to the center and turn it around
        Now around the gent and back we go
        Circle up four and here we go

(Head) Ladies Forward and Swing (8 beats)
When members of the same sex perform this basic, it is usually an elbow swing. Right elbows are hooked, weight is back, and a sustained, even turn is performed.

Call: Head two ladies forward and swing
        Swing around, give a swing
        Then get back home and swing your own
        Swing around at home

Left-Hand Lady Pass Under (4 beats)
Dancers are in the same formation as described in number three, page 25. Men two and four make an arch with their right-hand lady.

29

That lady moves slightly forward to enable the left-hand lady to pass under the arch and move to the next man on her right.

Right-Hand Lady High, Left-Hand Lady Low (4 beats)

Same positions as described above. Men two and four, holding the hands of both ladies, pull them forward to face each other. The right-hand lady holds her hand high, making an arch with the man to enable the left-hand lady to move under the arch and proceed to the next man. The right-hand lady, after making the arch, moves to the next man. This leaves the side men standing alone while the head men have two ladies, one on either side.

Call: Forward six and back
Up and back you go
With the right-hand lady high
And the left-hand lady low
Forward six and back (This may continue until number one lady is on her partner's right.)
Allemande left, promenade

Separate

The designated persons walk away from each other. The man goes left, the lady right. Wait for the next call which will indicate where to go.

Right and Left

Same as right and left thru.

Rip and Snort (12 beats)

All join hands. The designated couples walk down the center of the set passing under the joined hands of the opposite couple. Each person of the designated couple drops his partner's hand, and the lady moves to her right, the man to his left. They continue leading the rest behind them until they meet on the opposite side of the set where they join hands again. The couple that made the arch continue to hold hands. The man makes a right-face turn, the lady a left-face turn under their own joined hands and go completely around until the circle is again complete.

Call: All join hands and circle left
First couple rip and snort
Down the center and cut them off
The man goes left, the lady right
Join up hands and circle right

SELECTED DANCES CONTAINING THOSE
BASICS INTRODUCED IN CHAPTERS 3, 4

RCA Victor

Let's Square Dance, Richard Kraus, albums one through five

Educational Activities Incorporated

Honor Your Partner, Ed Durlacher, albums one through four

5

Basics Used in Posting

"Posting" is sometimes referred to as "grid work." In a dance involving this formation, the caller may begin with "Head two couples pass thru." From then on, all calls are directed to these couples though without further reference to them—"Dive thru, California twirl, square thru, and the like. The inactive couples, however, play a definite role in posting by acting as posts or props for the active couples to weave in and out of the set in various directions. The inactive as well as the active couples must concentrate on the calls because the active couples must move between the inactive partners; therefore, these people must separate and then move together again thus preparing for their own subsequent performance. The success of posting, then, not only depends upon the reaction of the active couples but also upon the alertness of the inactive couples.

Many of the basics described here are performed with a person other than the original partner. The concept of partner and corner must be understood, therefore, as a *position* and not as a particular person. A man's partner is always the girl on his right, no matter who she is.

Reaction must be made in relation to hand turn, turn, or direction. Dancers should learn to react to individual basics and not to their combinations. As the intricacies of the square dance unfold, it will become apparent that many combinations result from the simple addition of only one new basic. It is important that the student understand the mechanics of each. He should not anticipate but should merely take the required number of steps demanded by each call as one can never be assured of the nature of the next call.

In the hash call, the caller may begin with "Head two couples . . ." and continue to call basic after basic in meaningful and smooth combinations. A figure ends with an allemande left or with some other basic which signifies that all dancers should be in their home positions or back with their original partners, with all couples in correct sequence. This figure can go on indefinitely. This is the challenge of posting, both to dancers and caller, that attracts many people to the square dance. Excitement is generated by moving in and around the set, not knowing what will be called next, making use of skill and coordination, and finally arriving back in home position with all in correct order.

THE BASICS

In posting when number one man is brought back to his home position, all other dancers should also be in home position. The student should visualize a set while studying the figures used in this section. Follow the action of number one man as he walks through each basic.

Pass Thru (4 beats)

The designated couples walk forward, passing right shoulders with the person each is facing. The couples finish facing out. They do not turn around but wait for the next call.

Pass Thru, Separate Around Two (8 beats to separate around two)

After executing the pass thru, couples separate and move around two people. If the head couples perform this from their home positions, they will be back in their original position when finished.

    Call: Head couples pass thru

    Call: Separate around two

    Patter: Keep going around to home

    Call: Do-sa-do your partner

    Patter: Once around at home

Pass Thru, Separate Around One (4 beats to pass thru, 4 to separate)

The designated couples pass thru. "Separate around one" indicates that partners turn away from each other and walk around the nearest person. If the head couples perform this combination from home position, they will then be in between the side couples. When the heads perform this combination, side couples must separate from their partners in order to provide room for the head couples to move between them. Immediately

33

after the head couples have passed by, side couples move back toward their partners.

  Call: Head couples pass thru
      Separate around one
      Down the middle pass thru
      Split two and around one
      Down the middle, right and left thru
      Turn the girl around at home

Pass thru diagramed:

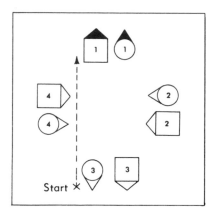

*Figure 1—Head Couples
Pass Thru*

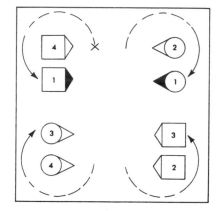

*Figure 2—Separate Around
One*

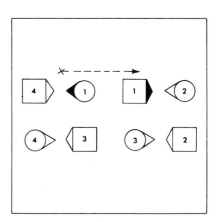

*Figure 3—Down the Middle
Pass Thru*

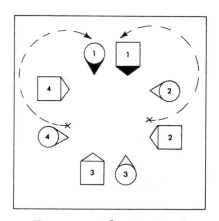

*Figure 4—Split Two and
Around One*

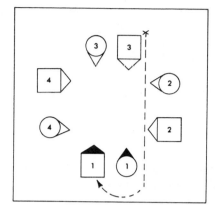

*Figure 5—Right and Left
Thru to Home*

The figure to the right makes use of the previously learned basics; however, in the call "Head couples pass thru, separate around one, right and left thru in the middle," the call "Right and left thru" will be performed with a person other than the original partner.

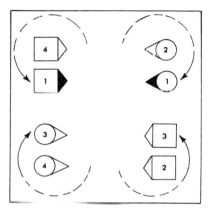

*Figure 6—Head Couples Pass
Thru, Separate Around One*

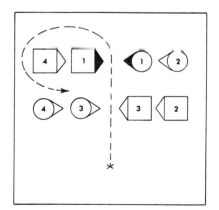

*Figure 7—Right and Left Thru
in the Middle: Start*

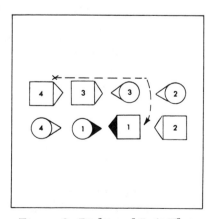

*Figure 8—Right and Left Thru
in the Middle: Finish*

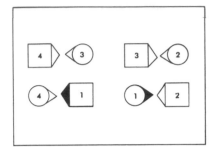

Figure 9—Pass Thru

Active couples now face their corners. An allemande left will take all dancers back to their partners and end the figure.

California Twirl (Frontier Whirl) (4 beats)

This is performed by partners (the woman on the man's right, the man on the lady's left). The man uses his right hand, the woman her left. Both begin facing in the same direction. Partners clasp hands and the man walks to his right as the lady does a left-face turn under the raised arms. The man walks behind the lady as she does her turn. Both should now be facing in the opposite direction from which they started.

Call: Head two couples pass thru
California twirl (These couples have achieved the results of a right and left thru.)
Heads pass thru
California twirl (All are now back in home position.)

Call: Head couples pass thru
Separate around one
Down the middle pass thru
California twirl (Instead of going down the middle of the set and performing a right and left thru, the couples pass thru and perform a California twirl, which has the same result.)
Pass thru
Allemande left (All are now in home position.)

In the next figure, the California twirl will not be called. It is used by the inactive couples without being told to do so when they find themselves facing out of the set. Partners do it naturally to get themselves back into position for the next call. This procedure is used continually during posting and thus is a *most important* concept to grasp. First, however, another basic is needed before explaining this movement.

Can you find two ways in which to bring number one man back to his home position?

Evaluation Question

BRINGING NUMBER ONE MAN HOME

e Chain (6 beats)

Two couples face each other across the set. The ladies walk toward other clasping right hands and walk by. The men wait until the en start down the set and then they follow. They meet the opposite and give her a left hand, walk by, and give the man a right. The comes with the lady facing out, the man directly behind her also in the same direction.

all: Head two couples right and left thru
Then Dixie chain in the middle of the night
The lady go left, the gent go right
Around just one, into the middle (Number one man has his back to number four lady.)
Box the gnat (Number one man has his back to number two man.)
Pull by, allemande left

Dixie chain, lady go left, gent go right around just one" is called, ers perform the same movement as in "Cross trail thru, separate ne."

hru, Four Hands (8 beats)

designated couples walk forward and extend right hands to the pposite. They walk by and make a quarter turn, men to the es to the left. Extending left hand to the next, they walk by, g to the right, ladies to the left. Extending right hand to the walk by. Men turn to the right, ladies to the left. Extending

Dive Thru (2 beats; when combined with pass thru, 4 beats)

One couple makes an arch. The couple facing them go under the arch. The couple that made the arch also perform the California twirl.

Call: Head couples pass thru, separate around one
Pass thru in the middle (The heads are now facing the side couples—number one man is facing number two lady and number three lady is his partner.)

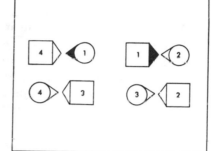

Figure 10—Pass Thru in the Middle

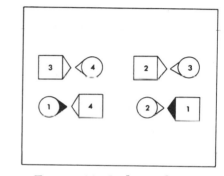

Figure 11—Right and Left Thru with the Outside Two

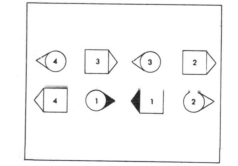

Figure 12—Dive Thru—Start

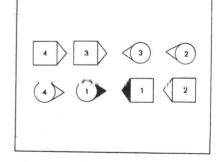

Figure 13—Dive Thru—Finish

Dive thru (The heads dive under the raised and joined hands of the side couples and are now facing in the middle. The side couples are left facing the outside of the set.)

It is here that the side couples execute a California twirl without being told to do so. This puts them back in their original position.

Students should practice performing the arch for the dive thru, California twirl until they react quickly to reaching for the partner's hand and to raising the arms while moving forward to perform the California twirl in four beats. The active couples take two steps to duck under and are then ready for the next call. Unless the California twirl is performed in correct timing, and this seems difficult for beginners at first, the next call cannot be performed immediately.

Cross Trail Thru (4 beats)

The designated couples walk forward, passing right shoulders with each other (same movement as pass thru). The lady goes left, moving in front of her partner. The man goes right, behind his partner. "Separate around one" often follows this call. Others could be called, however, so dancers must listen closely and should not anticipate the next call. Dancers often have trouble executing the cross trail thru. Remember, first pass right shoulders with the person you are facing and then cross over making sure that the lady crosses first.

Call: Head couples pass thru
Separate around one
Down the middle pass thru
Split two, and around one (Couples number one and three are on the opposite side of the set from their original positions.)
Cross trail thru, look for the corner
Allemande left

Box the Gnat (4 beats)

This is performed by two people who are *facing* each other. It is always executed with the right hand. Partners join right hands and the lady makes a left-hand turn under the man's raised right arm. The man walks forward. Couples end facing each other with hands still clasped. Partners have thus exchanged places.

Call: Head couples cross trail thru
Separate around one, into the middle (Number one man has his back to number two lady. Number three lady is on his left. From this position, it will be impossible for the active

couples to perform a right and left thru as m are not on the correct side of each other. F the gnat is called, the men and women t correct position.)

Box the gnat (Number one man now has hi four man. Number three lady is on his r
Right and left thru (Number one man no number two man.)
Pass thru, allemande left

Box the gnat may also be used in the following m
Allemande left
Box the gnat with your partner, pull by partners have hands joined. Pulling leaning back slightly, they pass rig other and meet the next person co this case, it is the corner.)

Allemande left
Grand right and left
Meet your own, box the gnat, pull
Allemande left, promenade your o

Box the Flea (*Swat the Flea*) (4 beats)

This is used to reverse direction using th indicated (the one *facing*), join left hands. turn under the man's raised left arm as the are now facing each other with left hands j

Call: Allemande left with your lef
Back to the partner and here
Box the gnat, pull by
Swat the flea, pull by (Rig partner.)
Grand right and left
Promenade

Dix

each wom lady finish facing

C

When " the danc around d

Square T

The persons o right, ladi men turnii next, they

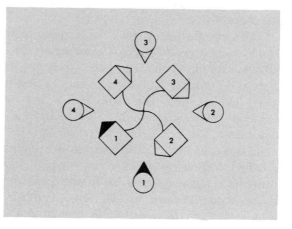

Diagram D:

BRINGING NUMBER ONE
MAN HOME

left hand to the next, they walk by. The quarter turn is *not* made after this last hand clasp.

A square thru, four hands, involves four hand turns; R, L, R, L. It is important to realize at this point that the hand clasps are merely used as guides. The hands are lightly touched, not grasped. After each hand turn, the men always make a quarter turn to the right and the ladies always make a quarter turn to the left. The only exception comes after the last hand clasp (left hand) when the dancers walk by and *do not turn*. If the head couples, starting from their home position perform this, they will end up facing their corner. Two steps should be taken for each hand turn. The rhythm is smooth and unbroken. What does the square thru four hands accomplish? In relation to the starting position, the men will end facing (quarter turn) to their left and the ladies will end facing (quarter turn) to their right. Presupposing that the couples started in home position, the active couples now should be facing their corners.

    Call: Head couples square thru four hands (Number one man is facing his corner.)
                Do-sa-do the corner
                Do-sa-do the partner

    Call: Head couples square thru four hands
                Right and left thru with the outside two (Number one man is facing number four lady, his corner.)
                Dive thru, California twirl (Number one man is facing his corner.)
                Allemande left

41

Star Thru (4 beats)

Two people facing each other perform the star thru. The designated people walk forward toward each other. The man raises his right hand, palm toward this lady. The lady raises her left hand and places her palm against the man's. The lady makes a left-face quarter turn under the raised hands while the man passes her with his right shoulder and makes a quarter turn to his right. That lady is now on his right. Both now face in the same direction.

Assume that the head couples are facing each other when star thru is called. Following number one man, it can be seen that he will perform the same movement as in the pass thru. After that movement, he makes a quarter turn to his right. Number two lady also performs the same movement as required in executing the pass thru and follows this with a quarter turn to her left. As a result, number one man faces number one lady. Number one man, however, has number three lady as his new partner. (In this explanation, "same movement" implies "equivalent movement." Since a specific hand movement is used in the star thru, the two movements are not exactly the same; however, they have the same result, hence "equivalent movement.")

Call: Head couples star thru
　　　　Right and left thru in the middle (Number one man has
　　　　　　his back to number two man.)
　　　　Pass thru, allemande left

Call: Head couples right and left thru
　　　　Star thru (Number one man has his back to number two
　　　　　　man.)
　　　　Pass thru, allemande left

Slide Thru

This is the same as the star thru except that no hand turns are involved. Dancers merely move into the positions described above.

Square Thru, Two Hands (*Half Square Thru*) (4 beats)

This is a half-completed square thru four hands involving but two hand turns. Opposites walk toward each other, extend right hands, walk by, and turn. Men turn to the right and ladies to the left. Left hand to the next and walk by but *do not turn.*

Call: Head couples half square thru (Number one man is now
　　　　facing number two lady.)

Right and left thru
Dive thru, pass thru
Allemande left

Call: Head couples star thru
Half square thru (Couples are facing out of the set from their home positions.)
California twirl (Couples are now back in home positions.)

Square Thru, Three Quarters: Square Thru, Three Hands (6 beats)

This is like a full square thru except that it involves only three hand turns. Opposite right hand, walk by, men make quarter turn to the right, ladies to the left. Left hand to the next, walk by and a quarter turn. Right hand to the next and walk by but *do not turn.* This is equivalent to the movement performed in the California twirl. It merely reverses the direction of the men and women while still maintaining the same partners.

Call: Head couples square thru three hands (Couples are still in home positions, but facing out of the set.)
California twirl (Couples are now back in original position.)

Call: Head couples square thru four hands
Right and left thru with the outside two
Dive thru (Number one man has his back to number four man.)
Square thru, three hands (Number one man is now facing number four lady.)
Allemande left

Left Square Thru (8 beats)

This is the same as square thru four hands, but beginning with the left hand. Sequence of hand turns: L, R, L, R. (The left hand is now free.)

Call: Head couples left square thru, four hands (Left hand is now free.)
Allemande left

U-Turn Back (4 beats)

Dancers turn individually in place to face in the opposite direction. The man, therefore, does not have his previous partner. The man's partner is always on his right. A box the gnat can offset this if the original partner is to be retained.

43

Call: Head two couples pass thru
U-turn back
Pass thru
U-turn back (Dancers are back in home position.)

Call: Head two couples pass thru
U-turn back, box the gnat (Couples are now back in original positions, but are holding the hands of the opposite dancers.)
Right and left thru
Star thru, pass thru
Allemande left

HINTS FOR STUDENTS

The square thru may be performed for any number of hand turns. So far, the square thru four hands, three hands, and two hands have been dsecribed. There is one other which is sometimes used—square thru five hands, indicating that the dancers perform five hand clasps. A quarter turn is made after each of the first four hand clasps. On the last hand clasp of the square thru five hands, dancers walk by but do not make a quarter turn.

Analyzing the square thrus, it can be seen that the following are equivalent movements:

Square thru two hands—a star thru, pass thru
Square thru three hands—a California twirl
Square thru four hands—for the men, a quarter turn to the left; for the ladies, a quarter turn to the right.
Square thru five hands—a pass thru

Following these hints, the movement of a square thru for any number of hand turns can be determined. For example:

Square thru six hands—a star thru, pass thru
Square thru seven hands—a California twirl
Square thru eight hands—a quarter turn to the men's left
Square thru nine hands—a pass thru

And so on. A square thru 64 hands? This would merely accomplish a quarter turn to the men's left (and after all the dancing!).

Box the Gnat is performed with the person one is facing. Right hands are used and an exchange of position is made with that person.

California Twirl is performed with the partner. As a result, dancers will face in the opposite position from which they started while retaining their partners.

Star Thru is performed with the person one is facing and that person becomes one's partner. The men use their right hands, the ladies their left.

Timing for the Square Thrus
If the Head (or Side) couples perform the square thru, four hands from home position 10 beats are required:

> 2 beats to walk forward
> 8 beats to perform the basic

If the Head couples perform the square thru, two hands from home position 6 beats are required:

> 2 beats to walk forward
> 4 beats to perform the basic

If the Head couples perform the square thru, three hands from home position 8 beats are required:

> 2 beats to walk forward
> 6 beats to perform the basic

SELECTED DANCES CONTAINING THOSE BASICS DESCRIBED IN CHAPTERS 3 AND 5

Folkraft	F-1282-A	Marianne	Dick Leger
Windsor	4817	Matilda	Bruce Johnson
Sets In Order	161A	Sunday	Earle Park
"	141A	Lida Rose	Lee Helsel
"	F 117A	Skipping Along	Johnny LeClair
Top	25007	Steel Drivin Man	Ray Bom
"	25132	Tweedle Dee	Dick Leger
"	25107	Swanee River	Dick Leger
"	25137	Ideas	Chip Henderson
Grenn	25031	Winchester Cathedral	Earl Johnston
"	12048	Mack Is Back	Earl Johnston
MacGregor	2008	So What's New	Ken Anderson
"	2010	Tied Down	Jerry Helt
"	1023	Put On a Happy Face	Bill Ball
"	1091	Dominique	Tommy Stoye
Blue Star	1629	Cocain Blues	Larry Faught
"	1810	For Me and My Gal	Al Brownlee
"	1796	Even Tho	Jim Brower

Bogan	1173	Little Bitty Tear	
"	4104	We're Drifting Further and Further Apart	C. O. Guest
"	3477	I Saw Your Face in the Moon	Charley Bogan Joe Lewis
J-Bar-L	5001-A	Rockin' the Polka	C. O. Guest
Kalox	K-1011A	My Blue Heaven	Jerry Haag
Wagon Wheel	201	He Li Lee Li Lee	Billy Dittemore

6

Basics Used in the Circle and Star Formations

In the process of progressing in square dance movements, one builds on basics previously learned. The basics of the circle and star formations described in this chapter utilize and add to formations studied in preceding chapters.

BASICS: CIRCLE AND STAR FORMATIONS

Dopaso (20 beats)

Dopaso involves an allemande left with the partner, allemande right with the corner, and then an allemande left with the partner. The last hand turn must be fully executed so that all are in their original positions. Dopaso is performed when partners are meeting with the left hand, although many callers utilize it from the circle formation.

> Call: Four ladies chain across the set
> Turn the girls around you bet
> Star right back for a dopaso
> Partner left with a left hand round
> Corner lady with a right
> Partner left go full around
> Full around then promenade

Allemande Thar (Preceded by an allemande left) (not counting the allemande left, 16 beats for one; 32 for two).

Allemande left with the corner, right hand to the partner. All are now facing in the correct position for a grand right and left. Walk

47

by and extend left hand to the next person. Holding onto that hand walk slightly by and the men turn into the center of the set and form a right-hand star. They back the star up as the women (still holding hands with the men) walk forward. The star moves counter-clockwise. When "Shoot the star" is called, right hands are dropped. Partners walk around each other until they again face in grand right and left position. If another allemande thar is called, the same procedure is followed—right hand, walk by, left to the next, and form the right hand star. "Shoot the star." Partners walk half around and each now faces his original partner.

Call: Allemande left for an allemande thar
Go right—go left—
Form that star like an allemande thar
Back it up but not too far
Shoot that star for another thar
Go right—go left—
Form that star like an allemande thar
Back it up but not too far
Shoot that star and do-sa-do
Back to back and promenade

Call: Allemande left for an allemande thar
Go right—go left—
Form that star like an allemande thar
Back it up but not too far
Shoot that star and do-sa-do
Back to back and here we go
Four ladies chain across the set
Turn the girls then promenade

There are two other ways to break the star.

1. *Slip the Clutch*: The men and women drop hands. The women continue to walk forward while the men, maintaining their right-hand star, reverse their direction and walk forward. The call may be "Allemande left" as the next person is met or "Pass one girl, allemande left the next."

2. *Throw in the Clutch*: Men and women drop hands. Both walk forward. The women promenade around the outside of the set while the men move forward in a right-hand star. "Pass her once, meet again, turn her by the left hand round."

Seesaw (8 beats all around left-hand lady, 8 seesaw)

The seesaw usually proceeds "All around your left-hand lady," which is a do-sa-do executed with the corner. Coming back after performing this, partners execute a do-sa-do passing left shoulders (not right).

Call: All around your left hand lady
My goodness! what a lady
Seesaw round your taw
Loveliest gal we ever saw

JUST DIFFERENT WORDS

The following calls are occasionally found in dances. Many times, however, the caller may not use these terms yet will direct the dancers through the same maneuvers using more familiar terminology. For instance, in the "Promenade Red Hot," the caller may merely say:

Call: All join hands and circle left
Turn the right-hand lady, right hand round
Partner left, left hand round
All the way around
Corner lady, right hand round
Partner left with the left hand round
All the way around and then

The caller has thus directed the dancers through the same maneuvers without using the phrase "Promenade Red Hot." Many callers, therefore, do not consider this a basic but rather a combination of fundamentals. However, since the following are found in dances, they are included here so that they will be understood.

Promenade Red Hot (24 beats)

All are promenading around the set. On the call "Red Hot," the man pulls his lady in front of him. (He does not turn.) She now faces clockwise on his left. The man now faces his right-hand lady. He turns her with a right hand and then moves back to his partner and turns her with his left. Proceeding to his corner, he turns her with his right hand, then back to his partner for a left-hand turn (full around).

Call: Promenade but don't slow down
Promenade go round the town
Promenade, it's Red Hot

> Right-hand lady with the right hand round
> Partner left with a left hand round
> All the way, a full turn round
> Corners right with a right hand round
> Back to the partner with a half hand round
> Full turn around then promenade

Daisy Chain (36 beats)

This involves the same concept as the grand right and left. The dancers, however, progress forward with two hand turns and then turn back to make a hand turn with the person behind them. Forward again with two hand turns, then turn back one. The sequence is two alternate hand turns forward and one back, thus progressing around the set until the original partner is met or until the caller terminates the movement.

Call: Allemande left with your left hand
Right to your own for a Daisy chain
It's a right and left and turn back one
Right hand round the corner one
A left and right to a brand new girl
Now turn right back as you did before
Left hand around new corner
It's a right and left and turn back
Right hand round on the inside track
Forward again, a left and a right
There's your own, promenade tonight

Catch All Eight (12 beats)

Designated persons take right forearms and walk halfway around each other. Exchange to left forearms and walk a full turn around.

Call: Out to your corner catch all eight
Her by the right halfway round
Back by the left all the way around
Promenade when you come down

Suzie Q (24 beats)

Two couples, facing each other, walk forward and turn the opposite person with a right hand round. All are now facing their original positions. (This is most important.) Walk down the set and turn partner with the left hand. Go completely around so that all face in the direction from which they started. Walk forward and turn the opposite person right hand round. Walk back to the partner and turn by the left hand. Go completely around until partners are in the original position.

Call: Head two couples right and left thru
Turn on around for a Suzie Q
Opposite lady right hand round
Partner left, left hand round
Opposite lady right hand round
Partner left when you come down
Go full around and then
Cross trail thru
Allemande left

SELECTED DANCES CONTAINING THOSE BASICS DESCRIBED IN CHAPTERS 3, 5 AND 6

Top	25048	Square Dance Jubilee	Chip Hendrickson
"	25012	Sweet Georgia Brown	Vern Smith
"	25013	Dollar Down, Dollar a Week	Lou Hildebrand
"	25131	Down by the Ohio	Dick Leger
"	25116	Green Green	Chip Henderson
Grenn	12033	Kingston Town	Earl Johnston
"	12091	Square Dance Blues	Earl Johnston
Blue Star	BS-1591-A	Will She Ever Think of Me	Buford Evans
"	BS-1641-A	Down at the Roadside Inn	Al Brownlee
"	ACA-4146	Swing Your Baby Now	Marshall Flippo
"	DS-1610-A	Too Many Sweethearts	Andy Andrus
"	BS-1569	North to Alaska	Vaughn Parrish
"	BS-1644	Crazy Rhythm	Joe Turnor
Windsor	4837-A	Bye Bye Blackbird (Ruth Stillion)	Dave Taylor
"	4804-A	Fiesta (Ruth Stillion)	Bruce Johnson
Bogan	B-1115-A	Into Each Life Some Rain Must Fall	Nathan Hale
"	B-1127-A	Please Don't Talk About Me When I'm Gone	C. O. Guest
"	1198	April Showers	Cal Lambert
MacGregor	1015	Ain't We Got Fun	Don Stewart
Wagon Wheel	WW-302	Houston	Beryl Main

7

Basics Used in the Line Formation

To understand what is accomplished in the line (route) formation, visualize couple number one and note the relation of this couple to the number four and number two couples. In the formations described previously, all couples have remained in correct sequence: number one couple always with number four to its left and number two to its right. In posting, only two couples were activated, and if number one man was brought back to his home position, all other dancers were also in correct position. In the line formation, however, certain basics take couples out of sequence. The caller, therefore, must be aware of the position of number one couple in relation to number four and number two while making his calls because if he terminates a figure with an allemande left and promenade, he must be certain that the original corner will be used for the allemande left because dancers otherwise will be out of sequence at the termination of his call. (If number one couple is in correct sequence, number three will be also; therefore, in studying the material presented in this chapter, it will not be necessary to be concerned about couple number three.)

LEARNING THESE BASICS

In the illustrations and descriptions, follow couple number one to determine what is accomplished by the various movements.

Heads Lead to the Right and Circle to a Line (8 beats)
Head two couples lead to the couple on their right (number one with number two; number three with number four). Join hands and

Evaluation Question

Where would couple number one be at the conclusion of this combination: heads lead to the right and circle four, forward and star thru, right and left thru, star thru?

circle once around. The head man holding onto his partner's hand drops the hand of the lady on his left and leads the circle to a line. The head man ends nearest his home position while the line is in the side position.

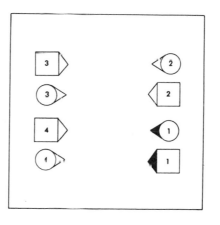

Figure 14—Heads lead to the Right. Head gents break to a line of 4.

Call: Heads lead to the right and circle four
Head men break to a line of four
Right and left thru (Dancers have exchanged positions with the couples opposite them. Couples are now out of sequence. They could not promenade to home from this position.)
Cross trail thru
Allemande left and promenade

53

Bend the Line (4 beats)

Couples are in lines of four. The center two people drop hands and back out to place holding onto the hand of the end person who pivots in place. If bend the line is used once, couples will be out of sequence. If repeated, all will be back in correct sequence.

Call: Heads lead to the right and circle four
                Head gents break to a line of four
                Forward up and back with you
                Up and back and then
                Forward again and pass thru

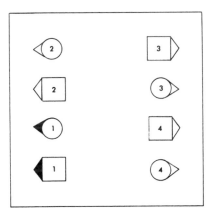

*Figure 15—Forward Again
and Pass Thru*

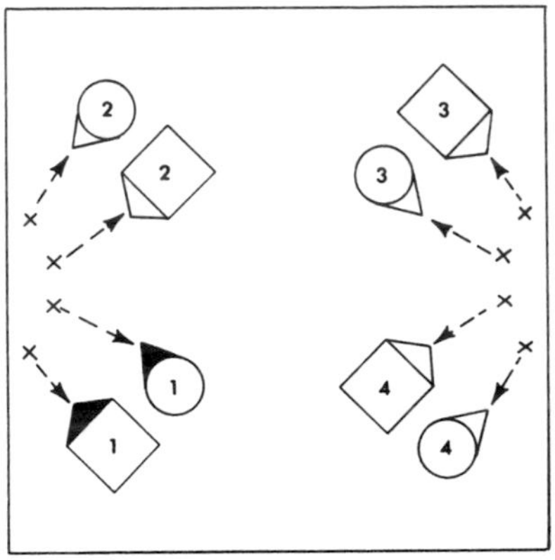

*Figure 16—Bend the Line:
Start*

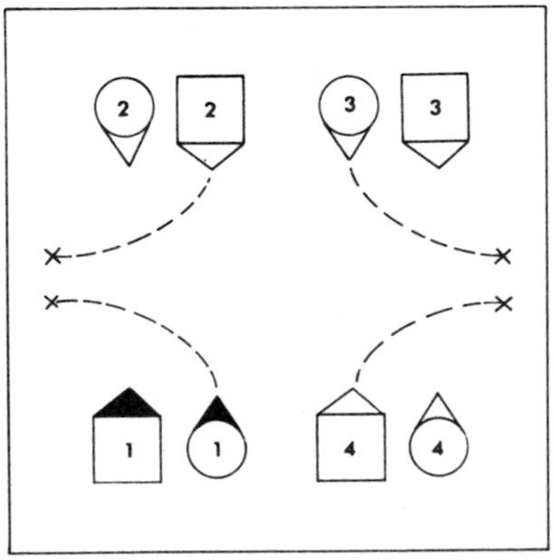

(Couples are now out of sequence.)
Call: Forward up and back
           Pass thru, bend the line

*Figure 17—Bend the Line:
Finish*

(Couples are now in sequence)
(Refer to Figure 18)

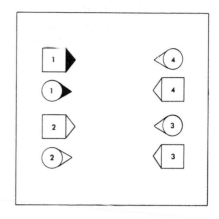

*Figure 18—Pass Thru, Bend
the Line*

Call: Right and left thru
Turn the girls around
you do
Cross trail thru
Left allemande, prome-
nade

Wheel and Deal (4 beats)
From a line of two couples, facing out, the couple on the right pivots around to face in the opposite direction. (The man turns in place as the lady walks around him.) The couple on the left of the line falls in behind the couple previously on their right. (The man pivots around the lady.) From a line of four facing out, there are now two couples, one behind the other, facing in.

Double Pass Thru (4 beats)
Two couples, one behind the other facing two other couples one behind the other, walk forward and pass right shoulders. Couples are still in a line, one behind the other, but are now facing out of the set.

Call: Heads lead to the right and circle four
Head gent break to a line of four
Pass thru
Wheel and deal, double pass thru
Separate, the first go left and the next go right
Form two lines and hold on tight (Couples are back where they were before the pass thru was called.)
Allemande left, promenade

When wheel and deal and double pass thru are combined and the "First couple go left, the next go right" is called, couples end in the same position in which they started, presupposing that the couples were in lines of four facing in when pass thru was called. This is a "zero movement," that is, no new position is attained thereby.

Wheel Around (4 beats)

Couples are in promenade position. At the call, they turn, as a couple, to face in the opposite direction.

Call: Promenade but don't slow down
Head two couples wheel around

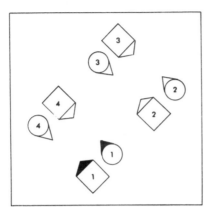

Figure 19—Head Two Couples Wheel Around

Call: Right and left thru with the two you've found

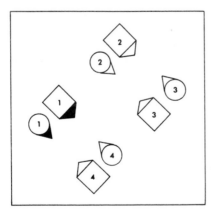

Figure 20—Right and Left Thru with Two You've Found

Couples are now out of sequence. In order to find the original corner, couples must be brought back into sequence. To accomplish this:

Call: Cross trail thru look for the corner
Allemande left

Other basics may be inserted:

> Promenade but don't slow down
> Head two couples wheel around
> Do-sa-do the one you've found
> Two ladies chain
> Chain back
> Right and left thru

Couples are now out of sequence. The following combination will put couples back in sequence again:

> Star thru, pass thru
> Allemande left

Couples may also be moved around the set:

> Promenade, etc.
> Head wheel around
> Right and left thru, right and left back
> Pass thru

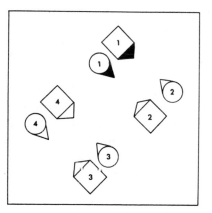

Figure 21—Couples Out of Sequence after Pass Thru

Couple number one is now facing couple two: however, couples are out of sequence. To find the original corner, the following combination (previously used in another figure) may be used.

> Star thru, pass thru
> Allemande left

Instead of passing thru to reach another couple, other basics may be used which, when combined, will result in a pass thru:

BASICS USED IN THE LINE FORMATION

Heads wheel around	Heads wheel around	Heads wheel around
Right and left thru	Right and left thru	Star thru
California twirl	Square thru 3 hands	Square thru 4 hands
Lead to the next	Lead to the next	Lead to the next

When couples are facing each other, as in the line or wheel around formations, it is possible for the caller to make such calls as the ladies chain, do-sa-do, and the like. These movements are simple but add a great amount of enjoyment to the dancing. When a caller wishes to terminate the figure, he must determine whether couples are in or out of sequence. If couples are in sequence, he merely has to call "Allemande left, promenade," and all will be brought back to home position. If couples are out of sequence, a "cross trail thru, allemande left, and promenade" or "Star thru, pass thru, and allemande left" will accomplish the desired results.

The same principle involved in the wheel around is applicable to the lines of four. For instance:

Heads lead to the right and circle four
Head men break to a line of four
Pass thru onto the next (couple one is now facing couple two).
The caller now proceeds as he did in the wheel around.

The student can see that very few 'new' basics have been used in this chapter. The line and wheel around formations do not involve intricate movements. It will be necessary, however, to become accustomed to moving as couples to another position in the set. Up to this time, as in posting, the square formation was used and the inactive couples acted as guide posts to keep the square in order. Beginners sometimes find this new formation difficult. To avoid problems, the man should always hold his lady's hand whenever he is not involved in performing movements with other dancers. The problem arises when, after combinations of basics have been called and partners (couples) are directed to a new position, the man moves correctly, but his lady, because of unfamiliarity with her position (and this could happen to the man also) wanders off by herself. If partners think in terms of *moving as a unit,* most difficulties in learning to dance in the line formation, will be avoided.

SELECTED DANCES CONTAINING THOSE
BASICS DESCRIBED IN CHAPTERS 3, 5, 6, 7

Top	25024	Billy Boy	Dick Leger
"	25070	Down by the Riverside	Chip Henderson
Grenn	12035	Big Daddy	Johnny Davis
Sets in Order	138A	Let a Smile	Bob Ruff
"	F113A	Sugar Blues	Johnny LeClair
"	148	I've Got a Hammer	Lee Helsel
"	165	One Dozen Roses	Don Schmelzer
Blue Star	BS-1638-A	Don't Expect Kisses	Andy Andrus
"	BS-1601-A	Sukie	Buford Evans
"	BS-1574-A	Walk Right Back	Marshall Flippo
"	BS-1596-A	Norman	Marshall Flippo
"	BS-1562-A	Lonesome Road	Andy Andrus
"	BS-1731	Careless Love	Andy Andrus
"	BS-1808	Wish Me a Rainbow	Andy Andrus
Bogan	BO-1138-A	Jambalaya	Joe Robertson
"	BO-1159	Puff the Magic Dragon	Billy Dittemore
MacGregor	992	Those Lazy-Hazy-Crazy Days of Summer	Chuck Raley
"	912	John Henry	Bill Ball
"	1036	Don't Let the Rain Come Down	Chuck Raley
Old Timer	8174	If You Don't, Someone Else Will	Jack Petrie
J Bar-T	4117	Walking My Baby Back Home	Joe Lewis
Jubilee	556	I've Got Bells on My Heart	Mike Michele
"	565	Just a Gadabout	Mike Michele
Kalox	K-1028-A	Walking to Kansas City	Billy Lewis
Windsor	4801	Living High	Bruce Johnson
"	4804	Cross Over the Bridge (Ruth Stillion)	Bruce Johnson
"	4813	Basin Street Blues (Ruth Stillion)	Bobby Peterson

8

Basics Used in Posting and Line Formations

Again, as in previous chapters, liberal use of illustrative diagrams are utilized to more effectively demonstrate movements required in the basics of posting and line formations. This chapter also builds on what has hopefully been well learned in previous chapters.

BASICS: POSTING AND LINE FORMATIONS

Ocean Wave (4 beats, if balance and ocean wave are combined)

With two couples facing, each person of these couples extends his right hand to the person each is facing and walks forward until right shoulders are nearly parallel. This leaves two people in the middle with left hands free. These dancers clasp left hands.

> **Call:**   Head two couples square thru four hands
> (The head couples are now facing their corners.)
> Ocean wave

The balance step is often used when this position is attained. All perform a two-step forward and a two-step backward. (Four beats). From this position, a right and left thru could be called. The right hands are already joined, so this is a natural sequence.

The ocean wave is a zero movement for no new position is acquired. It merely adds an interesting flair to the figure.

> **Call:**   Head two couples forward and back
> Forward again and do-sa-do
> Ocean wave

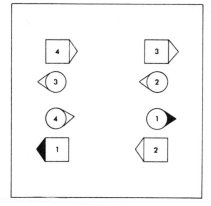

Figure 22—Ocean Wave

Balance forward and back
Right and left thru
Right and left thru again (All are now in home position.)

Circulate (All Eight, Just the Men, Just the Ladies) (4 beats)
    Call: Head couples square thru four hands

It will be noticed that the men are all facing in a certain direction, and, if they walk forward, or (if facing out of the set) walk to their right, each will take the position of the next man.

    Call: Ocean wave and balance
                  Just the men circulate

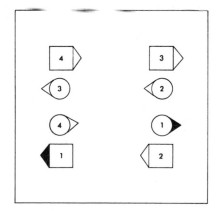

Figure 23—Ocean Wave

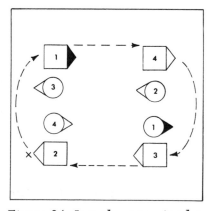

Figure 24—Just the men circulate

Call: Just the ladies circulate. (The ladies move forward, or, if they are facing out of the set, move to their left.)

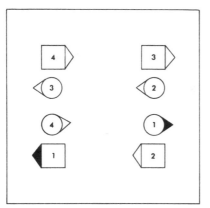

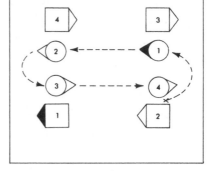

| Figure 25—Just the Ladies Circulate: Start | Figure 26—Just the Ladies Circulate: Walking to New Position |

In "All eight circulate," both the men and the women move at the same time. If performed twice in succession, all dancers will have moved to the opposite side of the set.

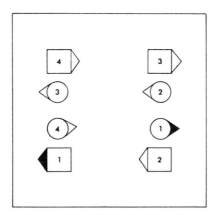

| Figure 27—All Eight Circulate: Start | Figure 28—All Eight Circulate (One) |

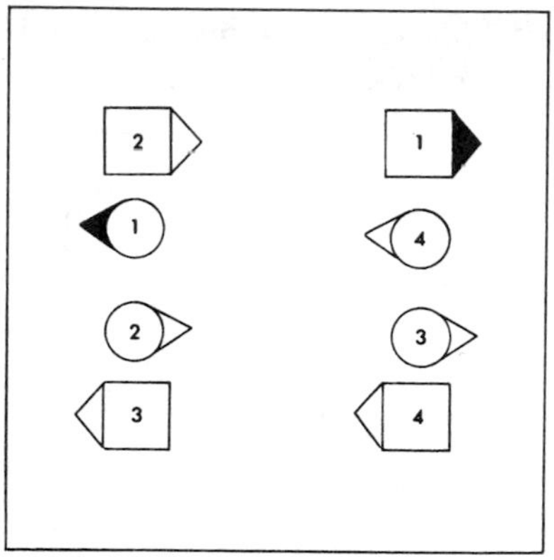

Figure 29—All Eight Circulate
(Two)

If "All eight circulate" is called four times, all will be back where they started.

Call: Heads forward and back
Square thru four hands
Do-sa-do
Ocean wave and balance
All eight circulate
Ocean wave and balance
All eight circulate (All are now on the opposite side of the set.)
Right and left thru
Dive thru
Square thru three hands
Allemande left, promenade

Swing Thru (6 beats)
Call: Head couples square thru four hands
Ocean wave and balance

All are now in position for the swing thru. The men are on the outside of the line, the women on the inside. The two in the middle drop hands (in this case, it is the women). On each end, two people are still holding hands. They walk forward (to their right), revolving in their positions while still retaining the line formation. This puts the women on the outside of the line and the men on the inside. Men and women drop hands. The men (or the two people in the center) clasp left hands. They make one more half turn until they reach the other lady. All clasp hands.

Number four man has his partner by the right hand, number one man has number three lady by the right hand.

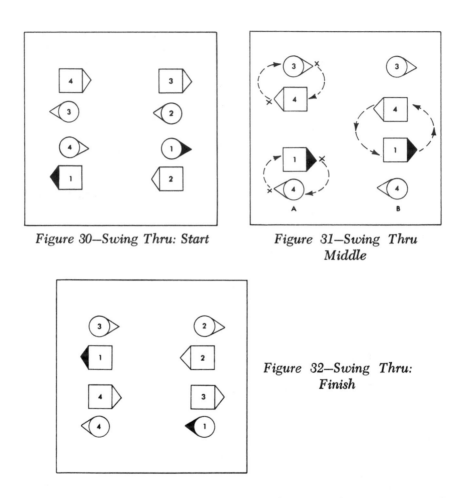

Figure 30—*Swing Thru: Start*

Figure 31—*Swing Thru Middle*

Figure 32—*Swing Thru: Finish*

It can be seen that the dancers are not in a position to perform a basic such as the right and left thru. However, if a"Box the gnat" is called, it would be possible to do so. If "Right and left thru" is now called, it would not be possible to effect the posting situation as number four man would have number three lady and not his original partner. If the caller uses a ladies chain at this point, the situation would be corrected. If two swing thrus are called in sequence, this would merely accomplish the same thing as a right and left thru.

Evaluation Question

Where would number one man be at the conclusion of this combination: heads square thru four hands, ocean wave, all eight circulate, ocean wave, balance, all eight circulate, swing thru, ocean wave, balance, swing thru?

Call: Head couples square thru four hands
Swing thru, ends turn in
Centers too, balance forward and back
Swing thru, ends turn in
Centers too, right and left thru
Right and left thru
Dive thru, square thru three hands
Allemande left, promenade

Notice that:
Two swing thrus result in a right and left thru.
Two all eight circulates manipulate all dancers to the opposite side of the set.
An ocean wave and balance is a zero movement.

Eight Chain Thru (16 beats)
Dancers must be in the posting formation to execute this call.
Call: Heads square thru four hands
Eight chain thru

Eight hand turns are required, and when the dancers have finished, they will be back in their original positions. Dancers will travel up one line and down the other. They begin with right hands, then alternate right and left with each succeeding person they meet. When dancers come to the end of the line, the men turn to the right and travel up the other side; the women turn left and travel up the other side. When finished, the right hand will be free. The eight chain thru is a zero movement.

Right and left thru
Dive thru, square thru three hands
Allemande left, promenade

Following number one man, trace his movements around the set:
Heads square thru four hands
Eight chain thru

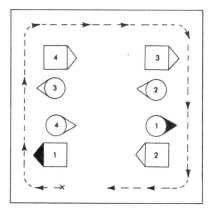

Figure 33—Eight Chain Thru

SELECTED DANCES UTILIZING THOSE
BASICS DESCRIBED IN CHAPTERS 3, 5, 6, 7, 8

Top	25113	Downtown	Ken Anderson
"	25129	Nobody Home But Me	George Peterson
"	25147	Be Happy	Bill Dann
"	25017	Bill Bailey	Vern Smith
"	25149	You're Nobody 'Til Some-body Loves You	George Peterson
Blue Star	BS-1649-A	My Ideal	Marshall Flippo
"	BS-1805	Love Makes the World Go Round	Andy Andrus
"	BS-1662	Is It True What They Say About Dixie	Vaughn Parrish
Sets In Order	162	Dream Boat	Bob Page
J-Bar-L	5006	Saturday Night	Joe Lewis
Jubilee	45-566A	Light in the Window	Mike Michele
Kalox	K-1040-A	Kissin' Cousin	Sam Mitchell
"	5-1069	I Used To Love You	Harry Lackey
"	K-1071	Cross the Brazos	C. O. Guest

MacGregor	1064	Pass Me By	Bob Van Antewerp
Old Timer	S-8141-A	The Battle of New Orleans	Bill Castner
Windsor	4870	Where Is the Circus	Wayne West

9

Unwritten Rules

All square dance basics and figures are not included in this book. A firm foundation should have been developed, however, if the dancer has become knowldgeable about the material which has been presented herein.

There is another aspect of the square dance which should be fully understood by all dancers. A set of unwritten rules—a code of etiquette—has governed the conduct of square dancers for many years. These "rules" were developed so that the attitude which prevailed during the barn dance era will not exist in the clubs and groups of people sincerely interested in good dancing. When one joins a square dance club, it will be expected that he does so with anticipation of dancing, that he enjoys the intricacies of the dance, that he is willing to spend the time required in learning to dance, that he appreciates moving to music in good timing, and that he desires to perfect his skill. Also expected is adherence to the following unwritten rules:

1. Clapping the hands and stomping the feet are actions which are discourteous to the caller and to other dancers because directions cannot be given or heard above this noise. This type of behavior is not accepted at square dances today. Listen attentively to the directions given by the caller. Dances cannot otherwise be performed correctly.

2. When mistakes are made, the entire set cannot perform the dance correctly. If mistakes are made in your set, however, do not show displeasure or impatience. Take time to help the person who does not understand. Remember, you also were once a beginner. Square

dancers are noted for their courtesy and helpfulness to others. If the square dance is to continue to embody the virtues of friendliness and acceptance of all, everyone must make an effort to practice these qualities.

3. If someone finds that he is below the ability of other dancers and therefore is not capable of performing the calls, he should remove himself from the dancing. He can enroll in a class to secure further instruction. He will have a much better time dancing with people whose level of ability matches his own.

4. As in any other activity, square dancers wear specific apparel. Men wear western shirts, ties, and pants. Women wear full skirts, petticoats (sometimes several), and dance slippers. This clothing allows freedom of movement and is very colorful (especially the women's), thus adding to the beauty of the dance. A beginning dancer may not at first want to spend the money for these costumes. Any type of clothing which permits free movement will be acceptable. Dungarees, tight skirts, heels, or boots will not be met with acceptance.

5. When a tip is over, every person in the set thanks the others with a handshake or a big smile and a "Thank You." This is the accepted method of ending the dancing at all square dances.

6. One never passes by a set in need of dancers to find another set where people are known or where better dancers can be found. Cliques are frowned upon. When attending a dance with other people, split up occasionally. One fine aspect of square dancing is the acquisition of new friends. Dancers may be assured that they can travel anywhere in this country, attend a dance, and feel perfectly at ease. This is an atmosphere which all square dancers desire to preserve.

These rules, simple acts of courtesy, are important. Participants are proud of their square dance clubs. They have found an activity where courtesy, love of dancing, and a relaxed, friendly atmosphere prevail at all times. When one participates, he will be expected to carry on this tradition. He will expect others also to abide by the unwritten rules which make square dancing one of the most popular, most challenging, and most enjoyable activities in the United States.

Sources of Square Dance Materials

RECORD COMPANIES

Blue Star, 323 W. 14th St., Houston, Texas 77008

Bogan, c/o Blue Star

Educational Record Sales, 157 Chambers St., New York, N. Y. 10007
    (Let's Square Dance Albums, and others)

Folkraft Records, 1159 Broad Street, Newark, N. J. 10011

Grenn, and *Top,* P. O. Box 216, Bath, Ohio 44210

Hi Hat, Box 69833, Los Angeles, Calif. 90069

Honor Your Partner Records, Educational Activities, Inc., P. O. Box 392,
    Freeport, New York 11520

J-Bar-L, c/o *Sets In Order*

Jubilee, 8811 N. 38 Dr., Phoenix, Arizona 85021

Kalox, 316 Starr St., Dallas, Texas 75203

Kimbo Educational Records, Box 55, Deal, New Jersey 07723

MacGregor, 729 S. Western Ave., Los Angeles, Calif. 90005

Old Timer, c/o Scope

Sets In Order, 462 N. Robertson Blvd., Los Angeles, Calif. 90048

Wagon Wheels, 9500 W. 53rd Ave., Arvada, Colorado 80002

Windsor, 5530 North Rosemead Blvd., Temple City, Calif. 91780

Scope, P. O. Box 64343, Los Angeles, Calif. 90064

PUBLICATIONS

American Squares, 1159 Broad St., Newark, New Jersey

Sets In Order, National Square Dance Magazine
    462 N. Roberston Blvd., Los Angeles, Calif. 90048
    Bob Osgood, Editor

70

Index